Nutty Nature

Chuck Whelon

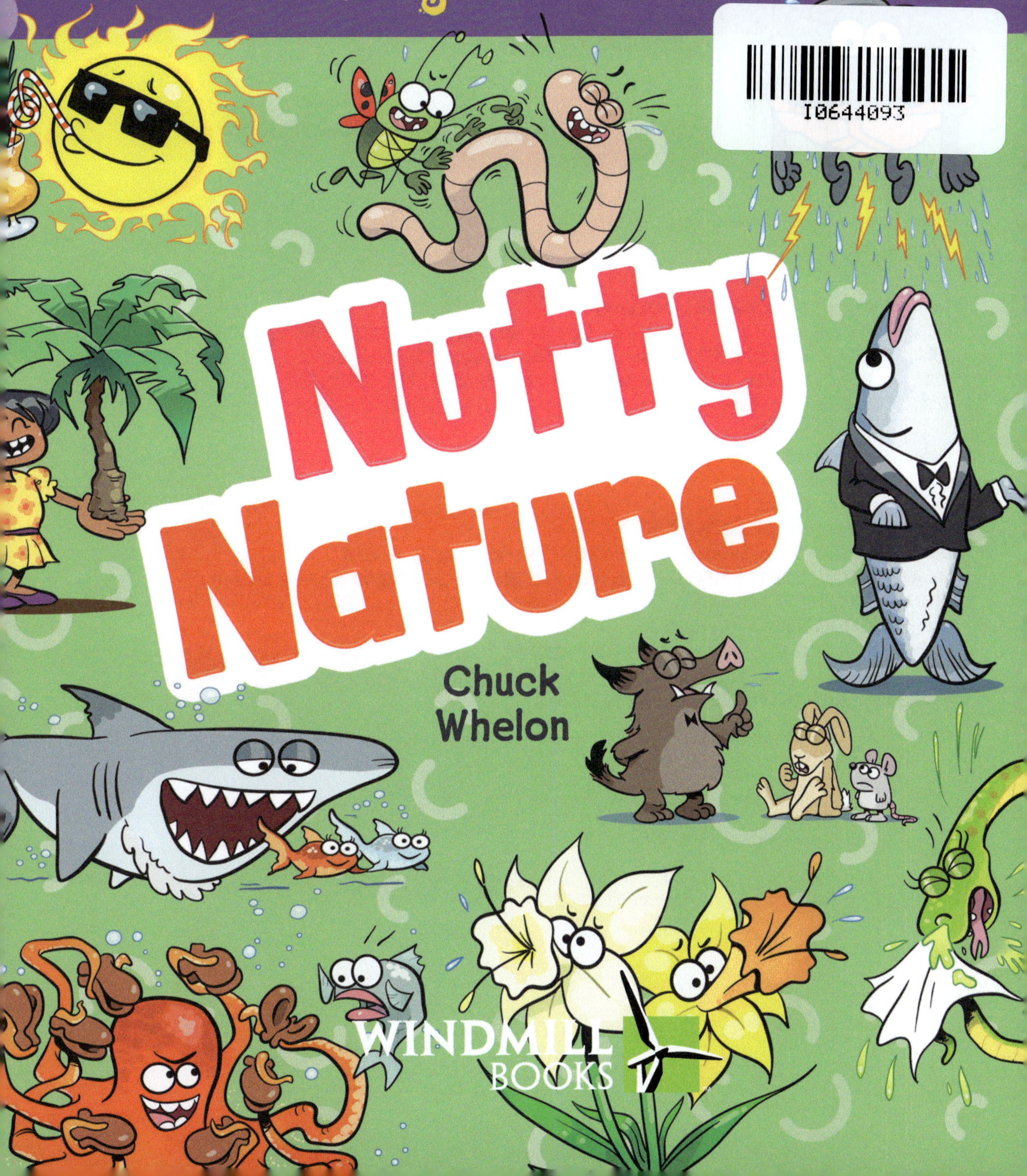

WINDMILL BOOKS

Published in 2019 by Windmill Books,
an Imprint of Rosen Publishing
29 East 21st Street, New York, NY 10010

Editors: Samantha Hilton and Joe Harris, with Julia Adams
Book Design: Stefan Holiland, with Emma Randall

Photo Credits:

Key: b-bottom, t-top, c-center, l-left, r-right
Chuck Wheldon: cover, 1, 3tl, 4bl, 5tl, 6bl, 7tr, 8bl, 9tl, 10tr, 11b, 12tr, 12b, 13b, 14tl, 15tr, 16bl, 17br, 18bl, 19tr, 20br, 21bl, 22tl, 32b; Shutterstock/Memo Angeles: 3br, 4cr, 5br, 6tr, 7bc, 8tr, 9br, 10bl, 11tc, 13tc, 14br, 15br, 16tc, 17tl, 18tl, 19br, 20tc, 21tr, 22br, 23tl, 23bl, 24tc, 24br, 25tl, 25bc, 26tl, 26br, 27tl, 27br, 28tr, 28bl, 29tr, 29bl.

Cataloging-in-Publication Data

Names: Whelon, Chuck.
Title: Nutty nature / Chuck Whelon.
Description: New York : Windmill Books, 2019. | Series: Joking around
Identifiers: LCCN ISBN 9781508195726 (pbk.) | ISBN 9781508195719 (library bound) | ISBN 9781508195733 (6 pack)
Subjects: LCSH: Nature--Juvenile humor.
Classification: LCC PN6166.W48 2019 | DDC 818'.602--dc23

Manufactured in the United States of America

CPSIA Compliance Information: Batch BS18WM: For Further Information contact Rosen Publishing, New York, New York at 1-800-237-9932

What did the tornado say to the plane?

"Want to go for a spin?"

How do snails keep their shells so shiny?

They use snail polish!

What did the cloud say to the bolt of lightning?

"You're shocking!"

What do you call a funny chicken?

A comedi-hen!

What part of the ocean is the deepest?

The bottom!

A pony went to see the doctor because it had a sore throat. "I know what's wrong," said the doctor. "You're a little horse!"

Why couldn't the snake say anything?

It had a frog in its throat!

What kind of clothes do storm clouds wear?

Thunderwear!

How can you tell that a cat likes the rain?

Because when it rains, it purrs!

Did you hear about the silkworms that had a race?

They ended up in a tie!

Riddle me this!

I often drop, but I never hit the ground. What am I?

The temperature.

What is on top of a snowman's bed?

A blanket of snow!

Why aren't trees good at quizzes?

Because they're often stumped!

What do cows do when they visit New York?

They go to see a moosical!

Why is it hard to tease a snake?

You can't pull its leg!

Riddle me this!

What is the largest moth in the world?

A mammoth.

What kind of tree can fit into your hand?

A palm tree!

What musical instrument are fish afraid of?

Casta-nets!

Try saying this three times, quickly.

Six silver swans swam silently seaward!

Knock, knock.

Who's there?

Cowsgo.

Cowsgo who?

No, they don't. Cows go moo!

Did you hear about the bee born in the spring?

Maybee ...

Why do male deer need to wear braces?

Because they have buck teeth!

What did the duck say after he went shopping?

Put it on my bill!

This animal wears a coat in winter, but in summer, it wears a coat and pants. What is it?

A dog!

Why don't oysters share their pearls?

Because they're shellfish!

Which sea creature eats its prey two at a time?

Noah's shark!

Why don't oysters like loud music?

Because a noisy noise annoys an oyster!

What did the vet give the sick horse?

Cough stirrup!

Why do penguins carry fish in their beaks?

Because they don't have any pockets!

What's worse than finding a worm in your apple?

Finding half a worm in your apple!

What do you call a mackerel in a tuxedo?

So-fish-ticated!

What do you call an ambitious wasp?

A wanna-bee!

What do you call a snake that works for the government?

A civil serpent!

Say this three times, quickly.

The six sick slimy snails sailed silently!

What sound do porcupines make when they kiss?

Ouch!

What do acorns learn at school?

Their tree times table!

Say this three times, quickly.

A big black bug blew big blue bubbles!

What do you call a deer with no eyes?

No i-dear!

What did the crab say to her grouchy husband?

"Don't get snappy with me!"

Why does the Moon wear sunglasses?
Because it's way cooler than the Sun!

Say this three times, quickly.
If you go for a gopher, the gopher will go for a hole!

What do you call a baby crab?
A little nipper!

Why wasn't the octopus afraid of being attacked?
It was well armed!

What did one raindrop say to the other?
"Two's company, three's a cloud!"

Why don't owls date during thunderstorms?
It's too wet to woo!

Why can't a leopard hide?

Because he's always spotted!

What's the best season to buy a trampoline?

Spring!

Riddle me this!

Go ahead and slice me apart ... you'll be the one crying! What am I?

An onion.

What lives in the forest and never stops talking?

A wild bore!

What does the sun drink out of?

Sunglasses!

What is in the middle of a jellyfish?

Its jelly button!

What is the biggest ant in the world?

The eleph-ant!

Knock, knock.

Who's there?

Toucan.

Toucan who?

Toucan play that game!

What kind of animal is the best at breakdancing?

A hip-hop-potamus!

Say this three times, quickly.

Swedish sword-swallowers swallow swords swiftly!

What do you call a woman who is good at fishing?

Annette!

What is a snake's best subject?

Hiss-tory!

What do you get if you cross a frog with a flower?

A croak-us!

Why don't fish ever win at poker?

Because of all the card sharks!

What do trees wear to the pool?

Swimming trunks!

Knock, knock.

Who's there?

Rhino.

Rhino who?

Rhino every knock-knock joke there is!

How do you describe an acorn?

In a nutshell, it's an oak tree!

What are the silliest flowers in the garden?

Daffy-dils!

What do you call a rabbit with fleas?

Bugs bunny!

What did the tree do when the bank was closed?

It tried another branch!

What did the bird say as it finished building its nest?

"That's the last straw!"

What do you call a man with pockets full of dry leaves?

Russell!

Knock, knock.

Who's there?

Bat.

Bat who?

Bat you'll never guess!

What do you call a man with a seagull on his head?

Cliff!

What should you do in the presence of a mighty tree?

Take a bough!

How do you get in touch with a fish?

You drop it a line!

Why didn't the viper wipe 'er nose?

Because the adder 'ad 'er 'andkerchief!

Which animal can jump higher than a building?

All animals can ... because buildings can't jump!

Why do you call that reptile "Tiny"?

Because he's my newt!

What is a myth?

A female moth!

Say this three times, quickly.

Two tiny tigers took taxis into town!

What does a lion say when he's introduced at a party?

Pleased to eat you!

What's orange and sounds like a parrot?

A carrot!

Riddle me this!

I am most useful when I'm broken. What am I?

An egg.

Cindy: It's really raining cats and dogs today.

Mindy: I know, I just stepped in a poodle!

Say this three times, quickly.

How many clams can you cram in a clean cream can?

What month do lumberjacks like the best?

Sep-timber!

What's full of holes but holds lots of water?

A sponge!

Who stole the soap?

The robber ducky!

What do you call a bear in wet weather?

A drizzly bear!

How can you tell a worm's head from its tail?

Tickle the middle, and see which end laughs!

No matter how much it rains, I never get any wetter. What am I?

A lake.

What type of bird works on a building site?

A crane!

What do you call a T. rex with magical powers?

A dino-sorcerer!

What game did the cat like to play with the mouse?

Catch!

What do horses wear at the beach?

Clip-clops!

Did you hear about the snakes that argued?

They agreed to hiss and make up!

Where do fish keep their money?

In the riverbank!

What did the worm say to her son when he came home late?

"Where in earth have you been?"

What's black and white and red all over?

A sunburned penguin!

Say this three times, quickly.

I think extinct insects stink!

Why shouldn't you tell jokes in the Arctic?

The ice might crack up!

What dog loves to take bubble baths?

A shampoodle!

Which animals are caterpillars most afraid of?

Dog-erpillars!

What game do tornadoes play?

Twister!

How do you stop a rhino from charging?

Unplug it!

What happened to the snowman in the spring?

He made a pool of himself!

What kind of pigs know karate?

Pork chops!

Why did the sun go to school?

To get brighter!

What do polar bears eat for lunch?

Iceberg-ers!

Say this three times, quickly.

How much wood would a woodchuck chuck, if a woodchuck could chuck wood?

Why are dolphins so clever?

Because they swim in schools!

Try saying this three times, quickly.

Felix fries fresh fish for Friday's fresh-fish festival!

What do you call a bee that keeps falling over?

A stumble-bee!

What do you call a bee that is unhappy?

A grumble-bee!

Riddle me this!

I'm an insect, and the first half of my name is another insect. What am I?

A beetle.

Did you hear about the happy raindrop?

It was on cloud nine!

What do you get from a pampered cow?

Spoiled milk!

Riddle me this!

Feed me and I live, but give me a drink, and I die. What am I?

Fire.

What do you call a snake that builds houses?

A boa constructor!

What do you call a sheep with no legs?

A cloud!

How do you get rid of an annoying wasp?

Tell it to buzz off!

What do you call a girl with a turtle on her head?

Shelley!

What did the farmer say to the cow when she ran out of milk?

You're an udder failure!

Say this three times, quickly.

Can a toucan do the cancan? Can two toucans do the cancan, too?

Glossary

adder A venomous snake with a zigzag pattern on its back.

Arctic The snowy, icy area surrounding the North Pole.

boa constrictor A large snake that kills its prey by wrapping itself around it and suffocating it.

buck A male horned animal such as a deer, reindeer, or antelope.

card shark A professional card player.

civil servant Someone who works for a state department.

clam A soft-bodied animal that lives between two shells of the same size. Some clam shells can reach a length of 4 feet (1.2 m).

cloud nine Being on cloud nine means being in a state of perfect happiness.

crocus A type of flowering plant.

extinct When no members of a species are alive anymore.

gopher A burrowing, furry rodent.

mammoth An extinct, hairy, huge prehistoric elephant.

minute (adverb) Tiny.

school (dolphin) A group, or pod, of dolphins.

sorcerer A wizard.

stirrup One of a pair of metal loops that are fastened to each side of a horse's saddle. Riders place their feet in them for support.

tornado An incredibly forceful storm that is made up of a funnel of swirling wind that reaches down to the earth.

toucan A tropical bird with a large, bright beak.

tuxedo A dinner jacket, worn on formal occasions.

viper A venomous snake with large fangs and a broad head.

woodchuck Also called a groundhog, woodchucks are large rodents that live in burrows.

Further Information

Books:

Elliot, Rob. *Laugh-Out-Loud Animal Jokes for Kids.* Grand Rapids, MI: Revell Books, 2012.

King, Joe. *The Funniest Animal Joke Book Ever.* London, UK: Anderson Press, 2015.

National Geographic Kids. *Just Joking: 300 Hilarious Jokes, Tricky Tongue Twisters, and Ridiculous Riddles.* London, UK: National Geographic Kids, 2012.

Scholastic. *Animal Jokes (Gigglers).* London, UK: Scholastic, 2017.

Townsend, John. *Truly Foul and Cheesy Animal Jokes and Facts.* London, UK: Salariya Book Company, 2017.

For web resources related to the subject of this book, go to: www.windmillbooks.com/weblinks and select this book's title.

Index